PROJECT MANAGEMENT INTERVIEW QUESTIONS MADE EASY

The Job Seeker's Guide For Successful Project Management Interviews

Dr. Andrew Makar, DMIT, PMP

ISBN: 1481982621
ISBN-13: 978-1481982627

DEDICATION

To Dawn, for all you do.

CONTENTS

ACKNOWLEDGMENTS

Special thanks to Dawn Makar, Mary Ann Makar, Bill Griggs, Tom Wachowski, Tim Mackenzie, Conrad Diez, Kelvin Ringold, Surya Prakash and Rick Stephens for their feedback and encouragement to make this book better for project managers everywhere.

INTRODUCTION

Why You Need to Read This Book

If you are a business professional seeking your first project management opportunity or you are an experienced project manager looking more senior roles, this book will help you prepare for a successful project management interview. If you are a project manager looking to hire junior project managers, then this text will help you ask meaningful questions that demonstrate experience in addition to project management competency.

By following the 7 step interview process, you'll be well prepared for your next interview as well as have a list of job opportunities to pursue. The text is much more than just a list of relevant project management interview questions. If you just want project management interview questions, Google the term "project management interview questions" and you'll receive an exhaustive list that you'll never remember or practically use in an interview.

Project Management Interview Strategies ... Not Just Questions

Many of the books on the market today simply provide a list of project management questions and suggested answers. Providing a list of questions and responses to memorize and regurgitate is unrealistic and ineffective at best. This text takes a different approach and provides an interview strategy using a step-by-step approach to identify opportunities, prepare for an interview and successfully pass an interview without memorizing.

This book will teach you how to prepare your resume, find the right opportunity, pass the initial phone screen and prepare you for your on-site interview and the stages afterward. After following this step-by-step process, you will also have a list of additional job opportunities to pursue in addition to your next interview.

Download Your Free PM Interview Questions Templates

In this planning guide, you'll learn about the Career Contact Matrix and the usefulness of the Interview Preparation Mind Map. I've included electronic copies of both templates for your personal use at: http://www.tacticalprojectmanagement.com/interview-bonus

Download the templates and get started putting them to use for your next project management interview!

PREPARING YOUR PROJECT MANAGEMENT PROFILE

Is Your Profile Relevant?

How well does your resume and professional profile reflect the profile of a project manager?

Before you start applying for project management positions or professionally networking for the next project management role, take an honest look at your resume and your online profiles. Hiring managers and recruiters don't read resumes – they scan them. Hiring managers are not looking for your latest treatise on project management theory. They want to know if you have the skills for the job and would be a potential candidate for an interview.

Remember the goal of your resume and online profile is to get an interview. These are lead generation pieces for your personal brand as a project manager. Therefore, your resume should only be one to two pages in length. Like most lead generation advertising, a single page is sufficient to provide a call to action to call your for an interview.

Avoid writing an entire treatise of your work experience. It likely won't be read. Instead focus on formatting your resume with keywords that make scanning your resume easy. Executive recruiters, headhunters and recruiting teams wade through hundreds of resumes each year to answer one simple question:

Should I call this person for an interview?

Your resume should be designed to provide a resounding **YES!**

Recruiters are often managing multiple requisitions to fill open talent requests. Once recruiters find a potential candidate, they start calling. If you want your resume to get recruiters calling you, your resume needs to be written in the proper must-call-now-manner.

Ask yourself a few questions:

How well does the resume represent the background of a project management professional?

Does your resume reflect core project management experiences or positions?

Are the project management skills highlighted and easily readable?

Is your resume optimized for quick scanning?

Conduct Career Keyword Research and Update the Resume

When scanning a resume, recruiters look for keywords that fit with the specific position description. If I am looking for a program manager with human resource software as a service experience, I'm specifically scanning resumes that indicate program and project management expertise with functional knowledge with human resources. If the resume doesn't reflect the criteria, it will be skipped.

The best way to tailor your resume is to review the job descriptions of open requisitions. This isn't a huge secret but since recruiter screen by keywords, it only helps if your resume has the keywords for specific job requisitions and job postings. Search dice.com, monster.com or careerbuilder.com for all the different project management opportunities. Remember to tailor your resume to include the keywords and desired skills from the position description.

If the job requisition is looking for a project manager with earned value management experience and you have experience managing earned value programs, remember to list it in your resume. I don't advise misrepresenting your resume but rather ensure the criteria the recruiter is searching for matches the resume that you submitted to a given position. You'll need to be able to demonstrate past experience applying these skills so be prepared to tailor your experience to the position.

Consider including the following project management terms:

Project Management Job Titles
- Project Management Professional (PMP)
- Project Manager
- Program Manager
- Project Coordinator
- Project Analyst
- Project Management Office
- Project Portfolio Management

Key Project Management Skills
- Scope Definition
- Schedule Management
- Scope Management
- Change Request Management
- Issue Management
- Risk Management
- Financial Management
- Vendor Management
- Contract Management
- Quality Management
- Work Breakdown Structures
- Communicate Project Status
- Meeting Facilitation
- Business Requirements
- Business Case Development
- Budget Allocation
- Project Management Methodology
- Project Plans

Key Project Management Tools
- Microsoft Project
- Microsoft Project Server
- Earned Value Management
- Critical Path Analysis
- Primavera

- Agile Project Management

What if your resume doesn't reflect the experience?

If you are seeking your first project management job, then your resume's position history won't likely be filled with core project management terms. However, if your position history doesn't claim project management experience, you can create a Relevant Experience section and highlight past experiences that utilized project management skills.

For example, have you ever led a community project or non-profit group? Chances are you've demonstrated scope definition skills defining deliverables for an upcoming pig roast or demonstrated schedule management coordinating soccer schedules for an entire project team. If you ever planned a party, wedding or large scale social event, you can still represent those experiences in project management terms.

Remember - The goal is to simply get a phone call to determine if you are a potential candidate for the position.

Your resume is an advertising piece for you and the desired action is to get a call from the recruiting or hiring manager. The following resume formats can be considered to optimize your resume for keyword embedding and quick scanning. Formats for a recent college graduate and an experienced professional are listed below.

Sample Resume Sections

College Graduate
Education – List school, major and GPA

Skills – Include a bulleted list of relevant project management and position related skills

Relevant Coursework – Identifying the relevant project management coursework helps the recruiter confirm relevant experience. If there were key concepts applied in the course, list them here.

Experience – Ideally, college graduates have had internships or co-op positions that provide real world experience. Add specific project management keywords reflecting internship or leadership experiences

Leadership and Involvement – College provides opportunities for student leadership and demonstration of team development skills. If you led a team project, developed a fundraising program or coordinated events for an organization, then summarize the contributions with a project management viewpoint. Remember to include the relevant terms in the resume as many recruiting software tools will identify resumes based on keywords.

Experienced Professional

The experience professional has less of an education and coursework focus since the skills and experience provide the project management background. My preference for a professional resume format includes the following keyword rich sections:

Professional Summary – Write 2 – 3 sentences that summarize your project management experience across your career.

Skills – List all the relevant keywords that comprise your skills as a project manager. If you are a Microsoft Project expert, list the skill set in this section. If you've been proficient at cost management across a large-scale integrated program, list the relevant keyword in the skills section.

Key Contributions – This section is another opportunity to highlight your leadership and key accomplishments using specific project management keywords.

Education – List your various degrees and academic certificate programs

Certifications – Are you PMI certified or have other designated PMI certifications – List them

Professional Experience – Include project management titles in your position keywords

Update and Clean Up your Social Media Profiles

Marketing companies are compensated each month to provide reputation management services to ensure a corporation's reputation is kept in a positive light. Your own online social footprint should also be kept in a positive light so you can connect and network your way to your next project management job. Social media is a useful tool but it can also cause problems if you misrepresent yourself for the world to see. Below are a few social media profiles you should explore and keep updated.

LinkedIn

LinkedIn may be the 3rd most popular social networking site compared to Facebook and Twitter, but it should be one of your key landing posts to promote your project management profile. Since you've updated your resume, its time to refresh or create your own LinkedIn profile the exhibits project management professionalism.

Two areas that you should focus on include the Summary section and Skills and Expertise section. The Summary section in LinkedIn is your open space to introduce perspective employers to your project management skills. Below is a sample profile from my own LinkedIn account.

Sample Profile

Dr. Andrew Makar is an IT program manager with delivery experience across projects, programs and portfolios in Automotive, Software and Financial Management industries. He is an enthusiastic leader who effectively translates project management theory into practical application. In addition to his IT management role, he is an author, instructor, and lecturer on a range of project management topics.

Specialties:
Strategic Planning, Project Portfolio Management, Program management, Project Management Office, MS Project

LinkedIn Skills and Expertise

Take the skills that you identified from the resume and the specific job postings and add them to your LinkedIn profile. LinkedIn now allows the people in your network to endorse your skills and provider further proof to your project management skill sets. You'll quickly find others endorsing your project management skills and you'll have the opportunity to endorse others as well.

Adding LinkedIn Social Proof

Do you have a project management related presentation that you've presented for school or for a local PMI chapter? Consider adding the presentation to your profile using LinkedIn's SlideShare or Google Presentation feature. These features allow you to upload a presentation and embed the presentation directly in your profile. By adding a recent and relevant project management presentation to your profile, it further establishes you as a thought leader promoting project management best practices.

LinkedIn also allows you to list any publications or relevant blog posts. I frequently update my own list of publications to appear relevant in the project management market. If you run your own blog on project management, integrate it with your LinkedIn profile. Of course, use discretion when posting blog content, especially when it comes to work related material. Unless you have permission from your company to post a presentation about a work related project, keep the presentation to generalized concepts.

LinkedIn simply works. I've been successfully making connections with relevant project managers in the field and have been recruited for new positions entirely based on my LinkedIn profile. Use it to meet new contacts, ask questions and start networking with fellow peers in the field.

Twitter

If you have a Twitter account, take a few moments and ensure your Twitter biography includes a few words related to project management. If I am a recruiter or hiring manager reviewing your resume and you list your Twitter account, I will review it to see if you are participating in the project management field. You'll want to also ensure your Twitter feed contains a few relevant tweets about project management articles, thoughts and hashtags such as #pmot (Project Managers on Twitter). A recruiter may do a Google search on your name and if your Twitter feed shows up, you'll want to ensure your social media profile reflects a professional image.

I prefer to use Twitter specifically for business and to network with other professionals in the project management and entrepreneurship market. I tweet relevant articles, share relevant posts and ask questions on Twitter to interact with other project managers. I use Twitter to develop a following of people interested in what I have to say about project management. I don't use Twitter to let everyone know I'm going to dinner and drinks at the local bar where they have my favorite micro beer on draft. Keep those private network posts for your friends on Facebook.

Facebook

If you are a working professional, then you know to keep your Facebook account clean. If you are a college student seeking your first job in a project management role, remember to clean up any potentially embarrassing pictures of you. If your privacy settings are not setup correctly, the last thing you want to see is yourself in a toga when they do a Google images search on your name.

Change your security settings so the Facebook friends that you work with don't see your latest job search updates. Don't worry, you can always switch them back once you found a new job. Be sure to remove any slightly embarrassing photos of you. As your move further up the professional hierarchy, what you say at work and out of work on the Internet becomes more and more important. There have been many examples where elected officials have gotten into trouble with questionable content that they've posted on the Internet.

Don't get me wrong. These social media platforms are excellent ways to distribute information and build connections. However, you want to ensure your profile is professionally presented when recruiters and other professionals want to connect with you.

Prepare Your Elevator Speech

What is an Elevator Speech?

An elevator speech is a specific description of your background and skills succinctly summarized into a few powerful sentences. An elevator speech is designed to leave an impression and can be delivered with the span of an elevator ride – hence the name elevator speech.

Why do you need an Elevator Speech?

In a recruiting setting, the elevator pitch is a key tool to making introductions, "breaking the ice" in an interview as well as positioning yourself as a strong and competent leader for the organization. In nearly 18 years of working in a professional field, nearly every interview has started with a handshake, an introduction and the opening question "Tell me more about yourself."

How do you respond?

If you don't have a thoughtful and prepared statement, you will likely fill the room with awkward pauses as you "um" and "ah" your way to a less then effective description of your skills and background. I have also been in interviews where the interviewers fumble with starting the interview and this is a key opportunity to demonstrate confidence and communication using your elevator speech.

Elevator Speech Example

Experienced Short Form

I'm a PMP certified program manager with 18 years of delivery experience managing global projects and helping businesses improve their project management delivery. My strength is in organizing teams and applying best practices to execute successful programs.

Experienced Long Form

I'm a PMP certified program manager with 18 years of delivery experience managing global projects and helping businesses improve their project management delivery. My strength is in organizing teams and applying best practices to execute successful programs.

I've delivered projects across manufacturing, finance and consulting organizations in addition to teaching project management courses at a local university. I am also a published author on project management best practices and write for several project management magazines.

Limited Experience Example

If you are a recent college student or have limited project management experience, an elevator speech example could be:

I'm a Central Michigan University Honors graduate with a degree in Business Management and a minor in Project Management. As the Vice-President of the Student Government Association, I've managed small teams coordinating events and volunteer programs across campus. I'm seeking an opportunity to apply my leadership skill set and further develop my project management background.

The Elevator Speech formula

There are a variety of approaches to developing an effective elevator speech. In some situations, the elevator speech is used to solicit a follow up communication or business opportunity from the target audience. In this situation, you are preparing a simple statement that tells the audience who you are, what you do and conveys a key benefit. The audience should walk away with a good understanding of who you are, what you do and potentially how you could benefit their organization.

The elevator speech formula includes:

Step 1: Describe who you are

Step 2: Describe what you do

Step 3: How can you help the organization? What is the benefit of bringing you into the organization?

Step 4: Put it all together and practice

The elevator speech is a powerful tool because it professionally summarizes your skills set as well as provides examples of how you can help an organization.

Where to put your elevator speech?

Once you have your elevator speech prepared, you can include it in your resume, your LinkedIn professional summary and even your two-sentence Twitter biography. You can include the elevator speech in any online profile that asks for a simply biography. Instead of writing a rambling history of your professional work experience, the elevator speech summarizes your contributions and encourages recruiters to ask for more information.

Step 1 Action Steps

1. Review and edit the resume to include relevant project management positions and keywords
2. Create or update your LinkedIn profile
3. Update Twitter, Facebook and other social media accounts for a professional image
4. Start preparing your elevator pitch

FINDING THE RIGHT OPPORTUNITY

Your resume is updated and contains the keywords for specific project management positions. Your LinkedIn profile reflects the summary, skills and experiences of a project management professional and you've eliminated any questionable material on Facebook. - including the time your friends took a photo of your belly flop into a frozen lake for the regional polar bear dip. You've written a decent elevator speech and have practiced it enough that is sounds casual and unscripted.

The next step is to find the right opportunity.

Finding the right opportunity and receiving a fast response are often inversely proportional to each other. This is due to the fact that finding the right opportunity takes a lot of investment in time and energy. With each opportunity, you need to professionally present yourself, qualify the opportunity as the recruiter qualifies you and continue to search the Internet and your professional network for relevant contacts and opportunities.

The majority of positions I've found in my career have been through previous relationships rather than formal submissions to job boards. Submitting to job boards and corporate job sites can be a laborious process and a poor investment of time. Once your profile has been submitted, there frequently isn't a fast turnaround or any feedback that someone is actually looking at your resume.

This is why I prefer branching out to my professional friends and colleagues to find out what opportunities are in the market. During an economic downturn, I found myself "downsized" and despite submitting to

11

multiple job boards, the opportunity that turned out to be the best one was from one of my professional contacts. The lead worked out because I had actively maintained a career contact matrix and had maintained a professional relationship.

Career Contact Matrix

I've used this tool to help me identify opportunities, leads, and follow up on active conversations for the next career opportunity. It's a simple matrix that can track active opportunities and identify contacts for professional networking and follow up over a three- to six-month time period.

I developed a career contact matrix using a variety of formats including spreadsheets and mind maps. The career contact matrix consists of 9 simple columns including:

- Opportunity Status
- Opportunity Title
- Company
- Contact Name
- Contact Phone
- Contact Email
- Contact Job Title
- LinkedIn Profile
- Next Steps

Career Contact Matrix

Opportunity Status	Opportunity Title	Company	Contact Name	Contact Phone	Contact Email	Contact Job Title	LinkedIn Profile	Next Steps
Interview	Program Manager	Acme	B. Wayne	555-1212	bwayne@acme.com	Director IT	http://www.linkedin.com/in/bwayne	Mtg on Nov-22
Active Leads	Portfolio Manager	IBM	D. Grayson	555-1313	dgrayson@ibm.com	VP Services	http://www.linkedin.com/in/dgrayson	Call Nov 30
Active Leads	Senior Project Manager	Accenture	M. Spectre	555-1414	mspectre@accenture.com	Partner	http://www.linkedin.com/in/mspectre	Call Dec 2
3 Month Follow Up	TBD	Dell	P. Parker	555-1616	pparker@dell.com	TBD	http://www.linkedin.com/in/pparker	Inquire in 5 Months
3 Month Follow Up	TBD	Apple	S. Rogers	555-1717	srogers@apple.com	TBD	http://www.linkedin.com/in/srogers	Inquire in 3 Months
3 Month Follow Up	TBD	Microsoft	M. Watson	555-1818	mwatson@microsoft.com	TBD	http://www.linkedin.com/in/mwatson	Inquire in 3 Months
6 Month Follow Up	TBD	Consulting Company	J. Jameson	555-1919	jjameson@cc.com	TBD	http://www.linkedin.com/in/jjameson	Inquire in 6 Months
6 Month Follow Up	TBD	US Army	M. Cole	555-2020	mcole@us.army.mil	TBD	http://www.linkedin.com/in/mcole	Inquire in 6 Months
Professional Contacts	TBD	Recruiter	J. Chan	555-2121	jchan@recruiterrus.com	TBD	http://www.linkedin.com/in/jchan	Call every 2 months
Professional Contacts	TBD	Recruiter	E. Weiss	555-2222	eweiss@greattalent.com	TBD	http://www.linkedin.com/in/eweiss	Call every 2 months
Professional Contacts	TBD	Recruiter	C. Kroger	555-2323	ckroger@zettalent.com	TBD	http://www.linkedin.com/in/ckroger	Call every 2 months

With most opportunities, there are multiple contacts for the different positions as the candidate progresses down the interviewing funnel. By tracking the key contacts associated with each opportunity, you can follow up several months afterward. The opportunity status column is used to reflect Active Leads, Follow Up in 3 months, Follow up in 6 months and simply Professional Contacts

I also include the resource's LinkedIn profile into the matrix since it provides an opportunity to learn about the contact's professional and sometimes personal background. In an interview setting, referring to a past school, common hobby or finding any angle to build rapport is often helpful. I don't recommend connecting with a potential interviewer using LinkedIn until you have permission to do so. However, if their profile is public, make a note of it in the matrix so you can research the person's background and find some sort of common ground in education, experience or other public information.

I do recommend connecting with professional recruiters using LinkedIn since recruiters often post the type of positions they are looking to fill in their LinkedIn status. If you maintain an active LinkedIn profile, your status updates will also be sent to professional recruiters in your network. The Professional Contacts status is used to store recruiters and other professional resources that I want to keep in touch with on a semi-monthly basis.

Just like any sales cycle, some opportunities turn into qualified leads and other opportunities don't meet your need or interest. By maintaining a career contact matrix, you can refer to the past three to six months of contact and revisit these key contacts based on the changing market conditions.

By keeping in touch with your contacts, new opportunities can occur frequently and a timely phone call can open up an entirely new job opportunity. When you are seeking a position, you want to remain "top of mind" with your professional network so they will think of you and potentially refer you to an upcoming opportunity.

Another key benefit of an updated matrix is it becomes your emergency unemployment rescue kit. If you've maintained good contact with the recruiters who understand the needs of the market, you'll have an advantage over the competition. The war for talent is ongoing with job seekers and job providers assessing each other to find the right match. For passive and active job seekers, having a few useful tools such as the career contact matrix only helps navigate the path to the next career destination.

Finding The Next Project Management Job

Now that you've assembled your career contact matrix, it's time to find the networking events and the people to fill the matrix! The next time you get an email from a recruiter, remember to add them to your career contact matrix. You never know when you'll need to use it and you'll want to refer to it to keep a pulse on the market.

Project Management Job Sources

The Monster of All Job Posting Boards

I am going to assume you have already submitted a profile to careerbuilder.com and monster.com since they are two of the largest resume and job opportunity databases. Create a profile, submit your resume and setup relevant job email alerts. In actual practice, I've posted to many open positions and rarely received a timely response. However, if you're fishing for a project management position, you need to put as many lines in the water as possible.

LinkedIn Jobs

Since you've already created an outstanding professional profile on LinkedIn, use LinkedIn's search function and look for open jobs using a project management, project coordinator and other related project management keywords. LinkedIn's advanced search feature lets you specify the location and industry of specific positions.

LinkedIn Executive Recruiters

It doesn't matter if you're not an executive. Recruiters like to find executive placements since the commission is much larger based on executive salaries. However, recruiters and headhunters are in the people business. If they can find the right candidate for a client, they will still realize a significant commission.

Using the same advanced search feature, select the People option in LinkedIn and start connecting with the recruiters in your area. Since recruiters are in the people business, they will welcome another connection or an opportunity to chat. Now you may not have an executive background, but the recruiter will provide insight into the current job market and let you know about any specific requisitions or hiring opportunities.

Based on your connection with the different recruiters, add them to your career contact matrix and follow up accordingly. Even if you have a current position, checking in with the recruiters in your career contact matrix helps you keep a pulse on the market.

Discussion Boards

Project management discussion boards are additional active communities to connect with other project managers. The networking strategy relies on building connections first. Joining a discussion board and posting your resume or inquiring about a job isn't the best way to find a proper project management job. The discussion boards are thriving online communities and even though people are hidden behind the anonymity of the Internet, project managers should connect with one another offline to build better relationships.

As of this writing, LinkedIn has over 6000 project management related groups segmented by specialty and location that you can consider. For IT project management, I highly recommend Projectmanagement.com (formerly Gantthead) provides an active discussion board as well as its own social community network.

Twitter for Professional Networking

Twitter has been a surprisingly useful network for project managers. Instead of following the latest celebrity tweets, I use Twitter to connect with other project managements and business leaders who provide value to the market. I've used Twitter to ask questions of fellow project managers, share advice and promote worthwhile blog articles. I've also used Twitter to make connections online with people who can connect with me offline for more direct conversation.

There are two popular hash tags that project managers use on Twitter including #pmot and #PMChat. #pmot stands for "Project Managers on Twitter" and #PMChat is a hash tag for "project management chat". Fellow project managers follow these hash tags to monitor relevant news and announcements that are related to project management.

If you're looking for active engagement from project managers on Twitter, I recommend participating in the weekly PMChat. The #PMChat is a free, weekly Twitter chat that is conducted every Friday at 12:00 noon EST. #PMChat was a community idea created by Rob Prinzo and Robert Kelly which has become a beneficial resource to project managers.

#PMChat is an innovative way to connect with other project managers, get answers to specific project management questions, and obtain different perspectives from IT pros across the globe. Project managers can also earn professional development units (PDUs) for their PMI certifications by participating in the chat.

From a networking perspective, participating in #pmot and #PMChat conversations, help make introductions to other project managers in the Twittersphere. I've been able to leverage these relationships to work on other projects, gain additional feedback and seek advice.

Remember, you are participating in an online community and the first step is to build your network before pushing for job opportunities.

Now that I have solid relationships with some of the project managers on Twitter, I feel comfortable approaching them for any upcoming job opportunities.

The previous examples were all online activities to identify contacts for your career contact matrix. Even though we work in an increasingly online social world, tweeting and linking in with project managers can only go so far. You will have additional success meeting contacts offline and locally.

Local Staffing Companies

Staffing firms, temporary services and "contract houses" are similar to executive recruiting firms except they seek to place talented project managers in contract positions. Some of these contract positions can last for 3 months and others last for years as companies extend each contract year after year. Staffing firms typically offer contract positions rather than permanent placement, however some also offer permanent positions.

My preference is to work for a company with a permanent position since the benefits and career growth tends to be better. If you're starting out and need experience, I recommend starting with the contract firms. If you recently found yourself out of work, local staffing companies are a useful resource to get the revenue stream generated again. If you can't find a permanent placement project management opportunity, many of the staffing firms have positions that are contract-to-hire after a specific period of time.

To find local staffing companies, simply search Google using the term "staffing firm" or "staffing company". You'll quickly find a relevant list of local staffing firms. Once you have your resume in their database, you'll be notified almost weekly of new contract opportunities in your area.

Local Project Management Institute meetings

The Project Management Institute (http://www.pmi.org) has project management chapters in nearly every major city across the globe. Attend a dinner meeting, formal presentation and connect with your fellow peers in the project management industry. Networking dinners provide a chance to socialize, learn something new and find potential opportunities.

I don't recommend approaching someone, handing them your business card and asking about future opportunities. I've spoken at previous PMI events and a few people have approached me looking for job opportunities and it isn't well received. I'd much rather make a connection around a professional topic, learn more about your background and then determine if there is a fit in the organization or a relevant opportunity. People help out those they like and have a friendly relationship. Building those connections doesn't happen overnight, but a PMI meeting is a great place to meet other project managers to start the conversation.

Local Meetup Groups

Meetup.com is an excellent resource for professional organizations and social hobby groups. People search Meetup.com to find local communities that share common interests and there is a good chance there are project management related meetups in your town. I found 4 within a search of my Metro Detroit hometown. If there isn't a local meetup, you could always take the initiative and start your own meetup to share project management best practices. As the leader of a group, it positions you as an expert and a team leader.

Your Own Personal Network

All of these previous resources are "cold" leads. These sources all require an additional investment of time to build trust and rapport. I've found my past 3 project management jobs through professional connections that I maintained and kept in contact throughout my career.

Who do you know who can help you find the next project management role?

Make a list of all the people in your network who have connections to project management or in your industry. If they are part of your active network, let them know you are in the market to find a new opportunity.

People like to help those that they like since it is a way to "pay it forward". Chances are your or someone else had helped them along their career in the past.

Remember to Follow up and Check In

If you experimented networking through any of the aforementioned resources, you should have a career contact matrix full of names for current and future follow ups. I designed the career contract matrix to be an active tool and not just to be populated and put into a drawer. Networking works with active connections and takes an investment of time to foster meaningful connections. Remember to maintain these connections every few months over lunch, a phone call or a social event.

Nothing screams of desperation more that someone calling me and asking for a job lead when we haven't spoken or exchanged an email in over a year. I've received a few calls full of sincerity and past intentions of "keeping in touch" under the guise of seeking a position. People help those that they like and have a connection. The people who connect under false pretenses are quickly put on the "I'll see what I can do list".

One of my mentors, told me the importance of being "top of mind" when opportunities pop.
The project management offer doesn't always go to the most qualified person, rather it goes to the people who is "top of mind" at the time. In your networking, you want to stay top of mind with the people who have access to the job experiences and projects you are seeking.

When I was looking for my first project management job, I met with select managers in different departments to learn about their projects and convey my interest in leading their next project. Eventually, an opportunity "popped", I got my first project and I've been building on each project management experience ever since.

Step 2 Action Steps

1. Download and start populating the career contact matrix at http://www.tacticalprojectmanagement.com/interview-bonus
2. Submit to 5 job board postings
3. Find 3 executive recruiters via LinkedIn
4. Connect with 5 professionals you haven't spoken with in 3 months
5. Ask a question about project management on Twitter and build connections
6. Once you have established rapport, inquire about opportunities

By following these steps, your inbox should be filling up with potential leads and your phone should be ringing with potential phone screens.

PASSING THE PHONE SCREEN

The next step in the project management job hunt is passing the phone screen. A recruiter or a Human Resources associate is typically responsible for identifying talent for a formal interview. They will reach out to you via email or a phone call to discuss your background and assess your fit for an interview. In smaller organizations, it may be the hiring member or a team leader making the phone call. The first call is an important one as it sets the stage for the next discussion and eventually your next job offer.

The Typical High Volume Recruiter Phone Screen

Professional recruiters have contracts with companies looking for talent. The recruiter typically receives a commission based on the position and salary of the candidate. Consequently, they screen hundreds of resumes and spend a brief amount of time with each candidate to determine if your resume is the next one to present to their client.

The typical recruiter phone screen follows this process:

1. Greeting

Hi. I found your resume online/in-a-job-bank and we have a position we'd like to discuss with you.

2. Brief Description of the opportunity for an employer who remains anonymous

Our client is a top tier manufacturer located in the Metro Detroit area seeking a

project manager responsible for application delivery.

For some reason, these recruiters fear being transparent and actually mentioning the client and the exact working location out of concern you will contact that employer directly and bypass their commission. I'm usually direct with these recruiters and simply ask what company is the recruiter's client. Some recruiters will balk at answering this question. Others try to provide just enough information that you can determine the hiring position.

3. Probe for fit

The recruiter may ask a few questions about your resume and do a check point to verify you actually use the project management terms on the resume. The recruiter likely isn't an expert in your field and is simply doing a scan of your resume and looking for validation that you use the keywords in your resume.

On numerous occasions, I've gone into specific detail only to be pushed through to the next question. At this stage, they want to validate you actually have the PM experience.

4. Validate interest

Based on your resume, is this an opportunity you'd be interested in?

If this is an opportunity you want to pursue, ask for a formal job description and indicate the interest. I get at least 1-2 emails per week that summarize steps 1-3. Some of these recruiters have resorted to using bulk email blasts with job descriptions to find leads.

5. The Salary Question

What is your current salary?

This question is often an annoying one as the recruiter who doesn't know you for more than two minutes is already asking sensitive questions that you only share with your employer and the government.

The goal of this question, despite your qualifications, is to screen you based on salary. If your salary fits within their pay range, they will purse the opportunity. If it is too high, the recruiter will quickly indicate that salary is too high based on the clients needs.

My strategy is to state my **desired salary range**. The recruiter doesn't need to know my current salary, but rather my desired salary range based on the compensation, benefits and any associated perks with the position. If they push your for an exact number, I still stick with a range which gives them enough information to know if you are candidate worth presenting and if the client can afford it.

Recruiters and human resources have a good pulse on the competitive salaries in the market. Large companies have established HR compensation planning directors responsible for administering and ensuring compensation packages are competitive with the market. There are entire compensation consulting companies like Towers Watson Wyatt specialize in compensation planning expertise. Chances are the company has an established range for the project management position.

If you do your market research, you can quote a range that is realistic for your experience in your local market. The range can be 10-15% of what you want your target salary and it should provide enough information to either include or exclude you from the candidate pool. Remember, the salary is always negotiable once you receive the offer.

6. Next Steps

Thank you for your time. I will review your qualifications with the client and get back to your shortly.

If this an opportunity you really want to pursue, be sure to have the recruiter send you their contact information and a formal job description. Add the recruiter to your career contact matrix and look forward to the on-site interview.

The Not-So Typical Hiring Manager Led Phone Screen

In other cases, the actual team leader or the hiring manager will be doing the phone screen. I've worked in small and large organizations where the hiring manager would do the initial screen and bring the candidate in for an on-site interview with other hiring managers. These types of interviews often come from campus recruiting teams or professionals who have attended career fairs seeking specific types of talent.

If a team leader or a hiring manager is interviewing you, expect some actual questions about your project management experience and details about your current projects.

1. Greeting
2.
Hi. I'm Clint Barton with Bow & Arrow Inc. I found your resume in our system and we have a position we'd like to discuss with you

3. Brief Description of the Actual Opportunity

We are seeking a project manager to help implement a new human resource and payroll system in our corporate office.

4. Project Management Background

Can you tell me a little about your background and your current project management work?

I always refer to my elevator speech since it is a strategic and meaningful introduction that highlights my contributions in a few sentences.

5. Actual Experience and Skill Related Questions

If a team lead or hiring manager is conducting the phone screen, you should anticipate direct questions about your skills and experiences from your resume. There is a strong possibility they are talking to you because they found a skill or experience that directly related to a project they are going to implement. It is difficult to directly identify the specific interview questions but if you look at your resume, you should be able to identify potential questions that related to similar projects in your industry.

6. The Salary Question

What are your salary expectations?

The interviewer may or may not ask this question. If they are the hiring manager or the team lead, they are looking for more of a functional fit than a financial one. In large companies, they will refer to the Human Resources department who actually makes the formal offer. I recommend using the same range guidelines as in the previous interview situation.

7. Next Steps

Thank you for your time. We will review our discussion and provide feedback shortly.

The same advice applies in this final step. Get the contact's name, phone number and email and ask for a formal job description. Add them to your contact matrix for follow up.

Working with a Executive Recruiters

If you are working directly with an executive recruiter, your experience will be more a bit more personal and hands-on. I've met with executive recruiters who have select positions available and they work to build a trusted relationship with both their client and you as the talent. Overall, I've found working with executive recruiters to be a better experience and they can help introduce your profile to the client so you are a "warm lead".

I got introduced to my first executive recruiter on LinkedIn. I created a profile and the company contacted me. We had a few conversations and developed a good communication around opportunities and expectations. The recruiter also had a good relationship with the client company and was able to position my credentials better than a cold call resume. Working with an executive recruiter who respects your skills and finds the right candidate for their client is an overall win-win.

The Phone Screen Desired Outcome

Remember the goal of the phone screen is to get you the next interview. You can use the phone screen to learn a little bit about the company and the opportunity. However, those meaningful details will be provided in the on-site interview and hopefully in the eventual offer packet. At this stage, just simply pass the phone screen and get to the next stage in the candidate evaluation process.

If the opportunity clearly isn't a match, be honest with the recruiter, explain it is not a fit for your career goals and move on. The recruiter may be screening on general project management skills versus trying to fill a specific position. Assuming you are interested in the position, you want the recruiter to pass your resume to the hiring manager and agree to schedule a follow up interview.

Step 3 Action Steps

1. Practice your elevator speech and be comfortable confidently explaining who you are in a few sentences.
2. Review your resume and brainstorm potential questions a hiring manager might ask about your background
3. Visit http://www.glassdoor.com or http://salary.monster.com for project manager salary ranges, benefits and total compensation
4. Establish your target salary range
5. Add any qualified recruiters as leads in your career contact matrix
6. Proactively talk to recruiters and hiring managers on your career contact matrix and schedule a few interviews.

PREPARING FOR THE ON-SITE INTERVIEW

You've successfully completed a phone screen and the recruiter has either emailed you or called to schedule an onsite interview. In this next step, you want to focus on establishing the interview mindset, understand the different types of interview formats, mastering the interview response and preparing for your upcoming interview with my favorite go-to interview preparation tool.

Understand the keys to a successful interview

The key to a successful interview relies on communicating how your skills and experience can help the organization while building rapport with the interview team. The hiring manager is assessing the candidate's skills while determining if the person is the right fit within the organization. Your goal in the interview is to best represent how your skills can help the project team solve their problems or challenges. You also want to determine how well the company is a fit for your own professional goals. The interview is a two-way street with you assessing the opportunity as the hiring manager assesses you.

Relax. It's just a conversation.

A common concern people have is overcoming interview anxiety. It is important to recognize being nervous is ok. People are evaluating you for a position you are interested in and within a 30 minute to hour long time frame, you are asked to justify and defend your knowledge and experience. It is important to remember that an interview is just a structured conversation. You may be competing against other candidates for the position, but it is still just a conversation.

Remember you are also evaluating the company and the opportunity. You may go into the interview and realize the corporate culture; the environment or the opportunity isn't the right fit for your skill set. That is perfectly fine. Remember the interview is just a conversation where each person is evaluating if the opportunity is the right fit for the person. Don't worry about trying to answer every single question correctly or if you fumbled the introductory handshake.

Relax.

You are interviewing them just like they are interviewing you.

Determine the Interview Format

When the recruiter calls to schedule an on-site interview, find out what the interview format will be and who will be participating in the interview. Interviews typically last 30 minutes to an hour and are with one interviewer or with a group of interviewers. When interviewing for project management roles, it is common to for the candidate to interview with the hiring manager, the department director and the project management office. I've also been a candidate for project management roles where I interviewed with the project team who would report to me in addition to the executive directors.

Understanding the interview format and who will be attending each interview will help you prepare for the interview and determine relevant questions for each participant. Knowing who will be attending the interview will help you understand the interviewers' roles and viewpoints on the position.

Conduct Interviewer Research

In preparation for the interview, research the interview participants using LinkedIn. As a potential candidate, the company may have researched your social media profiles and Internet footprint. Using LinkedIn to research interviewer profiles also helps you understand each participants experience and their time in each position. I've also used LinkedIn to find common ground to build rapport with the interviewers. You may find the participants had worked at the same company as you or attended the same college or are connected to someone you know well.

All of this information helps identify common ground to talk about in the interview and build rapport with the team. For project management roles, the PMP certification, past project experience and Microsoft Project mastery will help you get an interview. You ability to highlight these experiences while building rapport and helps interviewers see you as part of the team and will help you get the job.

Forget About Memorizing Interview Questions

It may seem odd that a book about interview questions is telling you to forget the specific interview questions. There are fundamental interview questions that are relevant to the project management position but they will vary based on specific role. The questions asked in a project management office role versus a program management role will be different. Even if you had all the questions to the interview, you likely wouldn't remember them all.

People don't hire you because you answer every question 100% correct. They hire you if they think there is a cultural fit with a qualified person who has the skills and relevant experience. Instead of focusing on exact interview questions, think about past scenarios and experiences. By reviewing past experiences that relate to the position, you'll be able to draw on other experiences to help answer any question.

Think About Key Project Management Scenarios

Project management can be divided into technical and management based competencies. The Project Management Body of Knowledge (PMBOK) provides a standards framework of processes, tools and techniques that define the technical side of project management. Scope management, developing work breakdown structures, managing schedules, tracking project budgets and reporting project status are all technical aspects of project management. The management side of project management includes the leadership, team building, customer management, negotiation and navigating politics within the organization.

Below are a few scenarios to consider.

Technical Project Management Scenarios

- How do you define project scope, gather requirements and support the scope management process?
- What is your experience developing work breakdown structures and managing project schedules?

- What tools have you used to effectively manage a project?
- How do you ensure a project has proper resources staffed for a project?
- How do you measure a project's progress?
- How do you communicate negative news to a project sponsor or executive management?
- What have been your experiences applying project portfolio management to a business segment?

Management Scenarios

- How do you facilitate problem solving within a team?
- Describe a time when you were responsible for resolving conflict on a team?
- How do you build teamwork across virtual teams?
- What actions do you take to ensure customer needs are managed throughout a project?
- Describe a time when you had to use peer influence to get work accomplished even though the people didn't report to you?
- How do you demonstrate leadership in your job?

These scenarios are all based on various technical and management dimensions. The questions are designed to have you reflect and think about your past experiences and align them to common scenarios in a project organization. By focusing on the different scenarios and your past experiences, you can direct any interview question to one of those scenarios.

The scenario approach is much easier to approach when preparing for an interview rather than trying to remember an exhaustive list of interview questions and the ideal response. Make a list of specific scenarios that relate to you resume and the technical and management scenarios. Review your resume and reflect on your past experiences. Think about the different projects where you've demonstrated both technical and management related competencies.

The PMBOK is also an effective resource to map experiences to potential questions. Scope management, risk management, integration management, financial management and other PMBOK sections are excellent areas for interview questions. Review your experiences and map your professional history against the PMBOK.

The next step is to practice a useful interview response format.

Crafting the Perfect Interview Response

I've spent 18 years on both ends of the interview table as a recruiter, hiring manager and job candidate. If you've attended an interview workshop or sought interview advice from job placement professionals, then you've likely heard of the STAR format.

The STAR (Situation, Task, Action, Result) format is an interview technique that simply works because it helps both the interviewer and interviewee to provide context around a project situation while providing specific actions and results. Many interview questions focus on situational questions where the hiring manager is looking for the candidate's rationale and past experiences solving similar problems.

The STAR format can be broken down into four parts:

Situation: The interviewer describes a situation or asks about a time when you found yourself in a specific situation.

Task: What were you trying to accomplish in the situation?

Action: What actions did you take given the scenario? What evaluation process did you use to select the specific action?

Results: What was the outcome of your actions? What were the key lessons learned from the situation? How have you applied this knowledge to future projects?

STAR Example

Situation: Describe a scenario where you had to balance competing customer demands with project constraints. How did you ensure customer satisfaction while maintaining the goals of the project?

Task: I was a project analyst supporting a new HR recruiting program. The program was responsible for re-engineering HR Recruiting operations and the first phase of the program involved launching a new best-in-class recruiting website.

Three days before the site was planned to launch, the HR director wanted to change the design of the website to include a full motion video welcoming the candidates the corporate website. This project was in the mid-1990s before high-speed Internet access was readily available. Most candidates were still using dial-up Internet access and a large full motion video on a corporate splash page wasn't technically feasible or realistic from a project timeline.

Action: I advised the director that due to the technology limitations and the timeline limitations, it wasn't feasible given the constraints. Adding a large video would actually hinder the user experience, as the user would be waiting for the video to download before even playing in the browser. As an alternative, I suggested we create an animated graphic of a waving hand that would still welcome the candidate to the website.

Result: The director liked the idea and agreed to the design change. I spoke with the development team and they agreed to the change request despite the tight timeline. The project continued to successfully launch on time and I was proud to see my little contribution on the corporate website. The key take away was to avoid any last minute change requests before a project launch date. However, it is the project manager's job to help manage the customer's expectations and find an agreeable solution.

Don't forget R is for Results

The results portion of the STAR formula is an important one to include. I've been in many interviews where the candidate provides background on the Situation and the Task assigned but they provide weak Action responses and forget the entire Results. Highlighting the actions taken at least conveys the response to the situation however; you want to complete the interview question with a clear description of the results and key lessons learned.

You want to provide a clear explanation of the task, action and results from your involvement in the scenario. Be proud of your results and how your involvement helped past projects. By adopting the STAR format, the interviewers will have a clear understanding of how you can help their organization given a similar context.

If there is still uncertainty or anxiety about the upcoming interview, let me reassure you that you already know the basic format if you think about it. The following is a simple 30 minute outline that actually demonstrates how you're in control of 30% of the interview.

The 30 Minute Interview Outline

By thinking about different scenarios and framing responses using the STAR formula, you'll be well prepared for the next interview. The next step is to anticipate the structure and flow of an interview. Your first project management interview may appear to be a mystery but if you think about the typical interview format it isn't too complex. The following outline is based on a 30-minute interview, although it can be applied to longer interview sessions. It is important to remember the key points you want to communicate in addition to answering the interview questions.

Introduction (5 minutes)

The introduction is a lot more than a greeting while looking the hiring manager in the eye with a firm handshake. Onsite office interviews are often scheduled in-between meetings during a manager's free time. Often, the interviewer may be a few minutes late or generally unprepared to start the interview. This is an excellent opportunity for you to direct the discussion with a brief summary of your background.

During the introduction, you want to recite your prepared elevator speech from Step 1 that summarizes your background and qualifications. I've used this approach several times when the interviewers struggled at initiating the interview questions. It is an effective approach to demonstrate initiative and confidence in the interview.

Position Overview (5-10 minutes)

The next five to ten minutes the interviewers will typically provide a brief overview of the project. Depending on the dialogue, the interviewers may go into additional detail before asking key questions. The next series of questions will try to determine how well your background fits the project. Remember to apply the STAR formula and respond with a description of the situation, summary of assigned tasks, key actions performed, and the action's results.

Relevant Experience (5 minutes)

After the project overview, the interviewers will likely ask about your experience as it relates to the project. Assuming you know a little about the project, you can reflect on your experiences and find a related example. If the project management position interfaces directly with clients or business customers, you'll want to highlight past experiences demonstrating how you connected with customers for effective delivery.

Technical Skills (5 minutes)

The title of "project manager" is often bestowed upon anyone in a leadership position despite their lack of technical project management knowledge. The technical project management question is intended to determine if you really know the science and not just the art of project management. This is an opportunity to highlight your technical experience performing critical chain analysis, calculating earned value, or resource leveling a project schedule.

Soft Skills (5 minutes)

The soft skill question is usually asked to test a project manager's team management skills and overall leadership behaviors. Look at your experiences and recall examples of conflict resolution, issue management, managing customer's expectations, and team building. You'll notice this technique focuses on experiences and not specific positions. Citing experiences from multiple positions is an effective technique to demonstrate breadth.

Wrap Up (5 minutes)

The last five minutes of the interview is your opportunity to ask any questions and inquire on next steps. Remember to reiterate your interest in the position and ask if there is anything else that requires further clarification.

Once you understand the basic interview format, there shouldn't be too much to worry about. In a 30-minute interview, you're controlling one-third of the discussion. You know at least one question will be related to the position and the other questions will address your project management background. The format should help remove any concern about potential interview questions.

Create Your Interview Preparation Mind Map

Keeping track of all this stuff can be a difficult to do. Remember you are not memorizing questions but recalling scenarios. I've found it helpful to organize the participant background, key questions to ask and refer to previous scenarios a mind map format. Creating a mind map on a single sheet of paper, allows me to perform a quick review of key thoughts and experiences, and relax knowing I'm prepared for the interview.

Organizing your thoughts in preparation for the interview can produce a combination of scribbles, scrawls and Post-It sticky notes all over your resume. Using a mind map to document your introduction, elevator speech, key experiences and questions will help you prepare for the interview. Here's a sample interview mind map:

The basic format of the mind map includes a section for interviewer information, company or project background, your introduction, elevator speech, and recent position summary. Additional topic nodes include a summary of technical management experiences and situational project management experiences. Each example branches into the STAR formula of Situation, Task, Action and Result. The format is simply a guideline. Expand the mind map for the key elements that fit your background and style.

The mind map is a quick and easy tool to prepare for an interview. Using the prescribed format and the mind map tool may not remove all pre-interview jitters, but it will help you prepare for a competent discussion. Since the mind map fits on one sheet of paper, you can quickly review your notes a few minutes before the interview and feel relaxed knowing you're well prepared for a successful discussion.

Mind Map Resources

There are a lot of resources available on mind mapping techniques. You can us a low tech approach with a sheet of paper and different colored pens. My preference is to use software tools to create the mind map as I like to update it for each interview. There are a variety of free and commercial software tools available to create mind maps. Rather than provide an exhaustive list of free and commercial tools, I'll recommend three for you to evaluate.

Xmind   http://www.xmind.net
MindGenius   http://www.mindgenius.com
Mindjet   http://www.mindjet.com

Xmind offers a free version that provides all the functionality you need to create a mind map for your next interview. MindGenius and Mindjet also provide excellent mind mapping functionality although these are commercial tools. Both provide additional functionality beyond the basic mind mapping structure. The paid tools also offer free 30 day fully functional trials of their software.

Step 4 Action Steps

1. Ask about the interview format
2. Research Interview names on LinkedIn and identify common ground
3. Brainstorm key project management scenarios
4. Practice the STAR formula
5. Review the 30 minute interview outline
6. Practice your elevator speech
7. Develop your interview mind map using the http://www.tacticalprojectmanagement.com/interview-bonus

INTERVIEWS MADE EASY

Welcome to the Big Show! You've reached a critical step. You've prepared and now you're ready for serious consideration. Remember, answering each interview question perfectly isn't required if you have the experience. Human Resources typically provides the interview questions to meet a compliance or corporate standards need. The interview is more about demonstrating credible experience and building rapport with the hiring team.

The hiring team is evaluating how well can they work with you while trying to determine how well you'll fit in the team. I've been on both sides of the interview table where the conversation turned into just a few professionals talking rather than answer every question perfectly. However, there are some core interview questions you should be prepared to answer.

Project Management Interview Questions

Staffing project management teams with capable and competent project managers is a challenge. If the interview isn't structured with effective questions, it can result in a poor hiring decision or a missed opportunity. Screening candidates on PMP certification is not enough to determine if they are an effective project manager. Due to the influx of PMP certification preparation courses, aspiring project managers can pass the PMP exam by taking a weekend course. The market has fostered a culture where certification is earned by training to a test rather than validating key leadership behaviors and technical competencies. Fortunately, the market doesn't base the hire decision only on certifications.

Over the years, I've used the following key questions to help staff my project and program management teams. The questions help identify competent project managers that understand project management theory and also demonstrate the practical application. The questions are grouped into two categories—leadership behaviors and technical competencies. Project managers need to demonstrate a balance between the mechanics of project management and the leadership qualities required to deliver the project. The questions are tailored for an IT project management interview; however, they could be modified based on industry. They are open-ended and will help shape the conversation.

Project Management Leadership Behaviors

Question #1: Describe a recent project where you were responsible for managing multiple people or teams. What were some of the key challenges and how did you handle those challenges?

Rationale: This question demonstrates a result-oriented leadership behavior. Project managers need to demonstrate delivery and a desire to attain the end goal. Staffing project managers who simply point out problems but do not help resolve them will not drive the project to completion. Effective project managers demonstrate how they've managed a project, coordinated across multiple teams, overcome obstacles and delivered the project's goals.

Question #2: Describe a time when you implemented a new idea without being asked or pursued a new opportunity that could improve the project or company.

Rationale: Demonstrating courage and a willingness to take action without being asked is a key delivery characteristic of effective project managers. Project sponsors entrust the project's goals, budget and their own reputations on their project managers. Project sponsors don't have all the
answers and need intelligent and motivated people to solve problems, identify new opportunities and take action without being prompted.

Question #3: Describe a scenario where you had to balance competing customer demands with project constraints. How did you ensure customer satisfaction while maintaining the goals of the project?

Rationale: Maintaining a customer focused approach while ensuring the project deliverables are completed on time is a delicate balance. Business partners don't understand all the technical details required to turn business processes into software solutions. They just want the system to work and accommodate their changing business needs. Effective project managers build rapport with their business partners, seek to understand the underlying needs and proactively address their concerns. It is a difficult balance as project managers commit to delivering the project scope while addressing a business customer's changing requirements.

Question #4: Describe a time when you had to balance quality management with a challenged project schedule.

Rationale: As projects execute and schedule variances occur, there is a tendency to shorten the quality testing cycle to maintain a project end date. In some projects, the end date can be extended, and in other projects, the end date must be maintained. Effective project managers recognize the importance of quality management in the software development cycle and prioritize the test cases and test cycles that deliver the project's critical functionality. These project managers successfully commit to a quality mindset and ensure defects are resolved or mitigated. The project manager should also recognize the challenge of managing the triple constraint and maintain a commitment to quality. Recognizing delays in the schedule early will help project managers adjust testing schedules so the support team isn't called in from a day off or a holiday.

Question 5: Describe a time when you had a difficult situation working with a vendor or another peer. What was your approach to resolve the issues while maintaining a positive relationship?

Rationale: Without a cohesive team, a project manager cannot be effective. Projects often depend on vendors and supplier team members to provide services. The nature of the client- vendor relationship emphasizes mutually beneficial goals. However, the vendor doesn't always prioritize the client's interests as heavily as their own. The ability to effectively develop teams across corporate borders is critical to project delivery. Clients will always try to maximize services at a minimal cost while vendors are motivated to increase costs for additional services.

In a challenged project with strained vendor relationships, it becomes even more important to focus on the critical issues to work together and deliver the end goal. The same skill is needed when working with other peers who are not necessarily motivated to help the project team. Strong relationships help solve problems and support project delivery. The best project management system, tools and techniques cannot replace the power effective relationships have across multiple teams.

Assessing Your Communication Skills

In this set of interview questions, there is not a specific question that addresses the project manager's communication skill or style. The open-ended questions provide the interviewer with enough feedback to determine how well the candidate communicates using verbal and non-verbal communication. Communication is 90 percent of a project manager's job, and interviewers should look for project managers who can logically and clearly respond to the interview questions as well as demonstrate project management theory in practice. These leadership behavior-based questions are just a few examples that identify a project manager's drive for results, commitment to customer satisfaction and focus on quality delivery.

Project Management Technical Competency Questions

Question #1: What steps do you follow to build a project schedule? How do you baseline a project schedule in MS-project?

Rationale: These questions assess the project manager's schedule development skills. The ideal candidate will walk through the steps to develop a project schedule including activity definition, sequencing, resource estimation, duration estimation and resource leveling. If the project manager can't tell you how or when to baseline a project schedule using Microsoft Project or another scheduling tool, then it is an early indicator the candidate lacks an important technical skill to execute the process.

Question #2: What techniques do you use to monitor and control project work?

Rationale: This question is used to assess how the project manager monitors the project, addresses schedule and cost variances, and controls the project through delivery. I'm hoping to hear the project manager schedules weekly project status meetings where project tasks are tracked against baseline dates and late tasks are reported. The interviewer should probe about the project management methodology, reporting techniques and any type of project metrics used to monitor and control the project. The candidate doesn't have to respond with the formulas for earned value management, but if they do, you know you've found someone who understands schedule variance and its impact on project delivery.

I have a personal bias to the importance of tracking and updating the project schedule. The project schedule is the key document that I use throughout all my programs and projects to ensure timely delivery. Project teams run the risk of missing key dates if they don't actively monitor and control schedule variance. If you're going to manage it, you need to measure it. Managing a project schedule provides the metrics to effectively manage progress. It is an administrative task, but it ensures the work will be tracked.

Question #3: Provide an example of how you've gathered business requirements for a project.

Rationale: In an IT project, effective project managers understand requirements definition and requirements management. Poorly defined requirements result in poorly designed applications. If requirements are not managed appropriately, the project's scope can grow out of control. Effective project managers have had past roles as business or systems analysts and can leverage those experiences to help gather business requirements.

Effective project managers can demonstrate usage of tools such as process flow diagrams, use case models, sequence diagrams and activity sequence diagrams to gather business requirements. A fully staffed IT project will have business and systems analysts available. However, effective project managers are knowledgeable in these techniques and tools and can apply them as necessary.

Question #4: Describe the project management methodology you have applied to your projects.

Rationale: This question assesses the project manager's knowledge of PMBOK or PRINCE based methodologies as well as how methodologies are tailored for a specific project. In IT projects, the systems development lifecycle (SDLC) and the project management methodology will be intertwined. Effective project managers know when to apply the various methodologies as well as align it to the supporting project management process. The project management question probes if the candidate understands that the SDLC methodology is the tool to deliver the project, while the standard lifecycle phases of Initiate, Plan, Execute, Control and Close support the chosen methodology.

Question #5: Describe the processes and tools you have used for quality management.

Rationale: This question focuses on the quality management aspects within a project. The project manager may have a quality lead or test manager responsible assigned to the project. In an IT project, it is important for the project manager to understand the software testing process and the tools used to support software testing.

Project managers don't need to be an expert in requirements traceability, unit, system, performance or user acceptance testing, but they should be knowledgeable in the process and its importance to delivering a quality product. At a minimum, project managers should understand requirement traceability from requirements definition through user acceptance testing. Without the traceability, the project runs the risk of missing test cases for key requirements.

Question #6: Describe how you manage project issues and project risks.

Rationale: Just like schedule management, the mechanics of issue tracking and issue resolution is an important success factor in project delivery. Project issues and risks need to be maintained in a project log and reviewed for action and resolution.

Candidates may respond that issues and risks are tracked as part of the project; however, the interviewer should probe for evidence of a review process. Effective project managers review the issue log each week with the project team and report the top issues with each status report. If the issue is logged and reviewed, project teams will not lose sight of the challenges requiring resolution.

Project managers should also describe how they identify risks, quantify the impacts, assess the probability and identify risk response plans. Risk identification and assessment workshops may be periodically conducted or at least reviewed as part of project status. Risk management is easy to overlook as teams are challenged with meeting schedule dates, creating deliverables and resolving project issues. Effective project managers will log the issues and risks, track their progress and continue to work the log. It is an administrative task that still needs to be performed to monitor and control the project.

Interview Questions You Should Ask

The interview should be a two-way dialogue about the opportunity. It shouldn't be a one-way battery of questions so you should feel comfortable asking specific questions about the project management opportunity. If this is indeed your next big opportunity, you want to ensure it is a right fit for your own career goals. Better yet, you don't want walk into a project and be surprised at all the rat holes and problems. There are going to be problems. That's what you are there to fix.

Below are a few questions to ask the interview team to learn more about the project. Depending on the position description, you'll adjust the question to the project or the project opportunity.

- What are the top three issues or challenges with the project that need attention?

- How well engaged are the business partners in the project or the portfolio?

- What is the make-up of the team or am I building the team from scratch?

- Is there sufficient budget in the project? Any contingency?

- Are there any government or regulatory constraints on the project?

- What does the career path look like for a project manager in your company?

Interview Pitfalls to Avoid

Nerves and being grilled with questions for an hour can be unsettling. Interviewers understand nervous jitters. Interviewers don't understand unclear responses or answers that reflect all theory and no practice. If you followed the advice in preceding chapters, you'll do fine. Below are some pitfalls to avoid:

Don't forget the R in STAR formula

The Situation-Task-Action-Result formula works because it provides everyone with an understanding of the assigned task and actions taken in a given situation. However, many candidates forget the Results portion of the formula. If you went through all the work to explain the situation, tasks and actions taken, don't forget to highlight the results.

If your previous actions resulted in a 500,000 savings to the project, mention it! The results are what people remember in an interview and they'll want to work with you to achieve similar results.

Avoid Generalities, Be Specific

I've conducted interviews where the responses had been filled with high level descriptions of project management terms. Simply restating text books terms or quoting the PMBOK isn't sufficient for a successful project management role. Avoid generic terms and provide specific examples.

If you managed an issue log and facilitated a change control process as a project analyst, be specific and share a few key issues or summarize the scope of a specific change control item and its impact to a project. By getting specific it provides better discussion and engagement as well as generates more open ended questions.

There is No We…It's About You

In an interview, you don't need to diminish or be humble about your accomplishments. We are often told to deliver as a team and take credit as a team.

-We delivered the project.

-We solved the technical problem that allowed the project to launch.

-We managed the customer expectations.

If a candidate uses "We" too much in an interview, it is unclear if the candidate did the work or simply was carried by the team. In an interview, your team isn't the room promoting your accomplishments so you need to represent yourself. There is no "We" in an interview, it is all about "You" and the talents you bring to the table.

Corporate Ignorance

I am consistently amazed at how many candidates I meet that lack any public knowledge about the company. I don't expect candidates to quote the quarterly balance sheet, but understanding the latest news, current product line, recent blog posts or mention the company's social media presence differentiates an active candidate from a passive one. In project management roles, you likely don't have "inside" information on the company's strategic roadmap, but demonstrating your interest in the company beyond its stock prices help solve corporate ignorance.

It also helps the interviewer see you as a fit for the position.

In addition to understanding the company's public presence, prepare questions for the interviewers. Some interviews had uncomfortable dead space and you can fill that dead space with thoughtful questions based on the research you did prior to the interview.

Don't Ask About the Money Yet

If you are interviewing for project management jobs, you've likely had enough interview experience to know the compensation information follows the hire decision. In the formal interview, avoid asking about the compensation. Present your credentials and demonstrate you are a fit for the organization and the money will follow.

If you're asked for a specific compensation number, stick to the range you provided the recruiter. Compensation and talent acquisition is an HR function. It likely isn't the responsibility of the hiring organization where you'll be performing project management duties.

The hiring organization may be able to influence Human Resources on the final offer amount, but you'll likely be negotiating it with Human Resources directly.

Step 5 Action Steps

1. Remember its about building rapport not answering every question perfectly
2. Review the interview questions in addition to your Interview Mind Map
3. Remember the STAR formula
4. Research the company prior to the interview
Develop interview questions for discussion

THANK YOU AND FOLLOW UP

After the interview, the next step is to send a thank you email to the hiring manager and follow up with the recruiter. I don't know why some candidates are reluctant to send a thank you email. I've never thought negatively of a thank you email. In fact, I've often thought it demonstrates initiative of a candidate who definitely wants a position. Sending a thank you email takes only a minute and also demonstrates a touch of class and respect for the hiring manager.

Finding the Email Address

In some interviews, the interviewers will give you their business card with contact information. In other interviews, you don't have the direct email and will need to figure out the format. If you were contacted by the company's recruiting department, then you should already have the email address of the recruiter. Figuring out the correct email of each interviewer should be easy if you know the email address format.

The Thank You Email

The Thank You email is a simple thank you acknowledging the interviewer's time and how you enjoyed the discussion. I reinforce the key strengths I bring to the company and reinforce my interest in the position. I've been in some interviews where the candidate just didn't seem to want the position. The Thank You email reinforces the interest.

Below is a suggested format:

Steve,

I just wanted to say thank you for your time today and the chance to learn about the opportunity with XYZ company. I know my strengths in PMO management and program management would be an asset to the project. The idea of joining the company in the program manager role is an exciting one. I look forward to hearing from you.

Thanks!

Andrew Makar

Recruiter Follow-up

If you were contacted by a recruiter who is different from the hiring manager or interview team, you'll want to follow up with the recruiter. I've found it helpful to let the recruiter know the results of the interview and encourage them to get feedback to you as soon as possible. Since executive recruiters and placement firms are paid a commission, they are equally motivated to find out about the position status. Developing a good relationship with the recruiter is also helpful when negotiating salary and benefits. The can act as your representative without having you facilitate the negotiation.

Step 6 Action Steps

1. Ask the recruiter for the interviewers' contact information.
2. If the contact information isn't readily available, try to figure out the email addresses based on the corporate email format.
3. Send a brief thank you email that reinforces your interest and key strengths
4. Follow up with the recruiter
5. Look forward to negotiating the offer!

NEGOTIATE, ACCEPT OR REJECT THE OFFER

Congratulations! You've completed the hardest part of the interview process. The rest is a waiting game to see if you are a fit for the position. Waiting for feedback can be frustrating but there is nothing you can do about it other than wait for the feedback. Below is some guidance on the Offer – No Offer outcomes.

The Offer

Now is the time for the happy dance! After receiving an offer decision, I readily admit fist pumping and demonstrating a Snoopy shuffle that would make Charles Schultz proud! It is an exciting time as you've demonstrated your experience and been accepted. All your hard work preparing for the interview has paid off and now you can enter the negotiation phase.

Why Negotiate?

At this point in the hiring process, you are in a strong negotiation position to increase your pay and benefits. Once you hire into the company, you'll lose some of your negotiation power. The company wants you and now is the time to negotiate for the best offer.

Salary

Everybody wants to be paid more for their work. Human Resources provides a market competitive offer based on their salary research and total compensation package. Remember salary is just one aspect of the total compensation. However, you should try to negotiate the salary higher based on your own industry research.

Back in Step 3, you researched salary profiles using sites like www.glassdoor.com and http://salary.monster.com. The research pays off in the negotiation phase because you can realistically compare the offer to the salary ranges found on other sites. My recommendation is to ask for 5-10% more of the original salary offer based on market research.

Salaries are usually allocated across salary ranges based on different quartiles. HR ideally wants each employee in the salary band to be in the middle rather than in the 1st or 4th quartile. Asking for 5-10% more will help you move across the quartiles but not necessarily push you into a new salary band. In large organizations, project management positions are aligned across different salary bands and the salary ranges may overlap between a 4th quartile project manager and a 1st quartile senior project manager.

Remember, it doesn't hurt to ask. Human Resources deals with negotiation every day. Ask for a little more and you may find the company will readily accept your offer. The alternative is waiting another 3 to 4 years of 2-4% merit increases to get the original 10% increase. HR can always decline your counter offer.

Bonus

If you are in a competitive market, you may be able to negotiate a signing bonus. If an annual bonus is associated with the position, you may want to negotiate a higher bonus target in exchange for accepting a lower salary. I prefer to get paid more throughout the year than wait for an annual company bonus, but it's a negotiation. By understanding what you want, you'll be able to negotiate the best offer.

Benefits, Vacation and Company Perks

Company benefits are usually assigned to each salary band. Executive salary bands have different benefits, vacation and corporate perks than management and non-management salary bands. Depending on the salary band, you may be able to negotiate the same salary but in a different band that grants you access to additional benefits.

One example is a colleague of mine was offered a project management role that did not include a company car benefit. By negotiating with HR, my colleague was able to maintain the same salary but get his job reclassified as a higher management role that qualified for the car benefit. Even though his salary and bonus were the same, his total compensation increased with the addition of a company car.

If salary and bonus are non-negotiable, I always try to negotiate an additional week of vacation. Adding an additional week of salary is like getting a 1.92% raise that isn't taxable. Vacation tends to be an easily negotiated item that doesn't cause the company much cost. Most projects can withstand an extra week of vacation and still maintain progress.

Accept the Offer

Assuming the offer is acceptable before or after any negotiation, the final step is to formally accept the offer and look forward to your new start date! Accepting a new project management offer is an exciting one because the work will be a refreshing new start and you no longer have to deal with the current project management baggage you're experiencing with your current project. Of course, there will be new project management problems around the corner, but take a moment and enjoy the victory.

Decline the Offer

In a competitive market with many qualified candidates, you may not receive an offer that meets your needs. It is perfectly acceptable to decline the offer and state your reasons why. You may find the company comes back with a counter offer. In other cases, the opportunity may not be a total fit for the salary and the work required. In this case, continue with your project management job search and repeat the process starting with Step 2. If you've been actively working your networking, you should have a lot of project management interview opportunities to consider.

No Offer

Ok. So it didn't work out. It is a disappointment. Remember, finding a project management job is a numbers game. It is a competitive market and there are a lot of talented resources. You may have been a fit for the role but there may have been other project managers willing to work for less compensation. In other cases, companies may interview many candidates but are simply not ready to make a hiring decision.

However, there is always another opportunity waiting in your network. Go back and repeat the process in Step 2 and continue identifying interview opportunities.

Remember to ask for feedback

If you don't receive an offer, I recommend asking the recruiter or contacting the hiring manager and ask for some honest feedback. It may be a long shot as most HR organizations provide a generic response. In other cases, you may get some realistic insight as to why you didn't receive the job.

One of my colleagues interviewed for an administrative job and made it to the 2nd round of interviews with the key decision maker. She didn't get the job and by following up with the hiring manager, she discovered all the candidates who were hired had a specific certification the organization valued. Knowing she didn't have the certification provided additional action steps for her to improve her resume and professional skills. She received positive feedback that she should apply again for a similar position and recognized the importance of obtaining the necessary certification. Unless she inquired, she wouldn't have known one of the key aspects of the hiring decision.

Just like the salary negotiation step, it never hurts to ask.

Step 7 Actions Steps

1. If you received an offer, try to negotiate a better offer
2. Accept or reject the offer based on the negotiation outcome
3. If you did not receive an offer, send an email to the recruiter or the hiring manager and ask for candid feedback.

THE FINAL WORD

I wish I could tell you there is a magic bullet for finding the right project management job. The reality is searching for the right job that meets your needs is a journey. By following this 7 step process, you'll increase your chances at finding and negotiating the best project management offer that meets your career goals. Finding the right project management job is a project in itself.

Remember to spend at least 1 hour a week on your career. This may involve improving your skill set for your current job or it may involve researching other opportunities where you'll find success elsewhere. You'll find better career satisfaction if you enjoy the project management journey, learning new skills and progressing from project and related job experiences.

Work isn't intended to be fun. That's why they call it work. However, managing your career contact matrix, interacting with other project managers and finding additional opportunities can add enjoyment to the day to day execution of project deliverables.

I wish you the best of luck in your project management endeavors and hope to learn about your project management interview successes!

BONUS MATERIAL

The following sections include additional interview questions and project management career advice from other project managers in my professional network. I encourage you to join the various project management forums mentioned in this book and engage with your colleagues on Twitter to discuss opportunities in our field.

Remember to Get Your Free PM Interview Questions Templates

In this planning guide, you've learned about the Career Contact Matrix and the usefulness of the Interview Preparation Mind Map. The electronic copies of both templates are available for your personal use at: http://www.tacticalprojectmanagement.com/interview-bonus

Download the templates and get started putting them to use for your next project management interview!

Ask the PM Practitioners

If you are interviewing for a future project management job, it always helps to consult with project managers in the field to get additional ideas on potential project management interview questions. A few years ago, I did some research across project management forums to identify useful project management questions. Special thanks to Han Robbers, Steve Rollins, Vasoula Chrioforides, Naomi Caietti, Rehan Ali and Subhashish Lahiri for their contributions.

Below are a few useful interview questions that other project managers have used in their interviews.

1. In the project, what activities will you spend 80% of your project time?
2. What added value do you provide to the project, customer or organization?
3. What is your strongest project management skill?
4. What project management skill is your weakest?
5. Do understand the corporation's core business?
6. What is your favorite leadership or management style?
7. How do you foster team development and manage team behavior?
8. How do you manage project delivery week-week?
9. Why should a team member want to be on your team?
10. What is your definition of project control?'
11. How do you measure project progress?
12. What is your experience managing multiple projects?
13. What are the challenges managing a portfolio of projects and how do you apply time management?
14. You are responsible for a project that is behind schedule and is missing major milestone dates and failing to complete project deliverables. What is your action plan to improve project performance and get the project back on schedule?
15. You've been assigned to a project with a fixed deadline, a limited budget and few resources. You realize you don't have enough budget to complete the entire project. How would you communicate the project status to the business sponsor?
16. How do you record risks before and during project executing? What is your plan for risk management?
17. How does critical path align with project objectives?
18. What project management leadership skills are essential?
19. How do you reward project team members on a project?
20. Have you been a part of a project that has failed? What lessons learned did you find?

These are just some of the project management interview questions you'll find on a variety of project management forums. If you have an upcoming project management interview, don't be afraid to post a question in the forums and get some practice answering the tough questions. It will help prepare you for future project roles.

Project Manager Career Questions and Twitter

Another useful resource for project management interview and career questions is Twitter. I've found Twitter to be a useful resource to get timely answers to key project management questions.

In the project management domain, there are a lot of books on how to pass the PMP exam and courses in project management theory. However, for students and aspiring project managers, there are few resources that provide career guidance on transitioning to a project management role, developing a core set of project management skills or putting the PMP into practice

Aspiring project managers often want to know:
- How did you get your first PM job?
- What is your best PM interview question?
- What are the top skills a PM must have?
- How important is PMP certification in your job?

For this book, I wanted to reach out to a few of my fellow project management colleagues via Twitter to get direct answers to these questions. Thanks to my colleagues at PMchat.net , I was able to get some quick answers. As you read through the responses, you'll see a few common trends as well as variety in project management responses.

Each response was limited to 140 characters or less so I bulleted them for easier reading.

How did you get your first PM job?

- Met with every manager in the building and asked about junior PM opportunities
- Doing a tech job, and someone asked me for a plan. Then they expected me to follow it.
- Spinning my process design, IT audit experience and convincing someone to hire me!
- I worked up from a developer to a Senior Dev and QA coordinator. A lot of the tasks were similar to PM. Got a job and took it.
- By accident! Boss noticed I had a talent for concept-to-completion projects and saw a need for that in our organization.
- Came up through the ranks in IT projects...analyst, architect, team lead, PM. Got the 1st PM gig when someone else quit.
- I did a very tedious task without being asked, saved money and a

lot of time in the end...I was the new PM :)

- Working a tech job just started documenting plans and processes using a framework and submitting to manager.
- Natural progression from Sr Developer to Team Lead to PM
- I fell into my first PM role -- opportunity came and I took it. Was previously a developer -> tech lead/architect.
- Got PM certification through my job and use it on the job, but job is technically not a PM job.
- Fell into it...self-taught most of the way, taking on progressively larger projects
- it came as part of my daily Job. ONE day you are a programmer, next a Team Leader, Project Leader, Project manager...
- Sometimes the PM path lies through content or business rather than tech.
- It sounds like people who "fall" into PM were first recognized for willingness to step outside their job desc. to add value.

What is your best PM interview question?

- When can you start? :)
- What value to believe the PM should add to the organization?
- Tell me about a project where you knew there was no way you could pull it off but you did, and how?
- What is the difference between a Project Manager and Project Leader?
- Explain how you deal with ambiguity and missing information in a project.
- We like to ask people about their experiences, and dig deep into how they've actually solved problems before.
- What do you do when team members don't cooperate?
- What is the role of methodology and tools in the PM space?
- Tough to pick one, but I like behavioral interviews in general. And always ask about a project failure
- Tell us about an experience when you had to resolve conflict. What was the nature of it and how did you deal with it?
- Tell me about a project failure. What type of techniques you used to keep it from falling off the rails?
- Then we ask "what if" questions to see how they respond to the unexpected: What if that hadn't worked? What would you have done?
- Good PM interview questions are more experiential. Need to

demonstrate HOW you have managed, not just give good answers.

- How do you keep your team aligned to project goals?
- Tell us about how you managed a difficult personality on your project team.
- Tell me about links between WBS, Schedule, Estimates and plan...
- How do you deal with people and conflict
- Talk about a project failure. If they say they never had any...questionable!
- What will you do in your first week as PM of this project?
- I have asked to see some of their actual project documentation...plans, communications, risk, etc
- What will you expect from a project sponsor?
- Is there a phrase that would be your vision for this project - Get 'er done, Team-driven development, Command & Control, etc?
- Do you see yourself as a taskmaster, or a delivery consultant?

What are the top skills a PM must have?

- Communication, conflict resolution, analysis.
- Leadership, organized personality and communication
- Negotiation, facilitation and analytic thinking
- Imagination, empathy, organization.
- Communication, leadership, enthusiasm
- Communication, negotiation, inspiration
- Communication, conflict management, team building.
- Communication skills (written, oral, presentation), organization, leadership
- Customer focus, business sense, people skills
- A PM should be disciplined, but flexible in the face of changing circumstances and competing priorities.

How important is PMP certification in your job?

- Useful - talked about study groups, offered to coach & develop staff to improve delivery.
- We value the PMP, but it is one of several more important factors we look at when hiring.
- Not at all.
- It was a Life changer. New opportunities, better salary, new friends
- I can't join a company now without having the certificate.
- I don't have it - not an obstacle until looking for new opportunities - certifications seem to carry more weight with some than

experience
- added value for job search
- Getting my PMP designation was not critical at all; the value's been more intrinsic to me/my knowledge.
- It was important in the transition from content PM to joining the tech PMO at my company. A big career boost.
- PMP is of limited benefit in UK. PRINCE2 opens more doors. Also Agile PMP is gaining traction.

Books and classrooms are excellent resources for project management theory and many classes do provide practical opportunities to apply project management. However, nothing beats getting real world advice from active project managers. Aspiring project managers, students and even experienced project managers can learn a lot from each other just by reaching out into one of several online project management communities including LinkedIn, Twitter and PMChat.

Below are the list of interview participants and their Twitter names. I encourage you to follow them as each provides their own unique view on the world of project management.

BenFerris	http://www.twitter.com/BenFerris
califgirl232	http://www.twitter.com/califgirl232
dwrichy	http://www.twitter.com/dwrichy
EdmontonPM	http://www.twitter.com/EdmontonPM
grandunifiedpm	http://www.twitter.com/grandunifiedpm
irivera	http://www.twitter.com/irivera
ITKevinW	http://www.twitter.com/ITKevinW
JCTAlexander	http://www.twitter.com/JCTAlexander
KellySolutions	http://www.twitter.com/KellySolutions
klkaz	http://www.twitter.com/klkaz
kmjs2002	http://www.twitter.com/kmjs2002
peoplepm	http://www.twitter.com/peoplepm
PersimmonGroup	http://www.twitter.com/PersimmonGroup
pickles_david	http://www.twitter.com/pickles_david
PPMpractitioner	http://www.twitter.com/PPMpractitioner
rkelly976	http://www.twitter.com/rkelly976
robprinzo	http://www.twitter.com/robprinzo
SaMoRaAli	http://www.twitter.com/SaMoRaAli

If you have additional project management questions, feel free to send them a tweet or join the community of project managers for another PMChat on Fridays at 12:00 Noon EST. Please visit www.pmchat.net for more details.

QUESTIONS AND COMMENTS

I'd enjoy the opportunity to hear your thoughts. If you have a favorite project management interview question, I'd like to include it in future versions of the book. Feel free to email me at:

andy@tacticalprojectmanagement.com

Feel free to also connect with me at the Tactical Project Management Facebook page at http://www.facebook.com/tacticaprojectmanagement. I often post useful project management articles, tips and relevant advice. More importantly, I want to learn about your project management interview successes!

Need Help?

I help aspiring and experienced project managers solve project management problems with a tactical project management approach. Connect with me and let me know how I can help with your next project! I often post new project management tutorials on my project management blog at www.tacticalprojectmanagement.com

Can you do me a favor?

If you believe the book is worth sharing, would you take a few seconds to let your project management colleagues know about it? If it turns out to make a difference in their career development or helps them hire better project managers, they'll be grateful to you - as will I. Please leave your review at http://amzn.com/B00ANEVZ0C

ABOUT THE AUTHOR

Dr. Andrew Makar is an IT program manager with delivery experience across projects, programs and portfolios in Automotive, Finance and Management Consulting industries. He is an enthusiastic leader who effectively translates project management theory into practical application. In addition to his IT management role, he is an author, instructor, and lecturer on a range of project management topics including PMO management, ERP implementation, application portfolio management and infrastructure management.

He frequently publishes on Techrepublic.com, ProjectManagement.com and additional published works have appeared in Projects@Work and Software Test and Performance Magazine. He is also an adjunct professor at Lawrence Technological University and Davenport University. When he isn't working, writing, or teaching, he's found playing with his kids and learning the occasional card trick or two.

Made in the USA
San Bernardino, CA
13 November 2015